PATTERN ACA
by CHAR

E-book

Pattern Drafting
Manual

For Drafting Patterns Based On Personal Measurements

Beginner Friendly Curriculum for Dressmakers

by **Ebere Benson-Ezeh**

E-book Pattern Drafting Manual

For Drafting Patterns Based On Personal Measurements

Beginner Friendly Curriculum For Dressmakers

Copyright © 2022 by Ebere Benson-Ezeh

Copyright © 2022 by Ebere Benson-Ezeh

Contents

INTRODUCTION

Hello there, my name is Ebere but my friends call me Eby, I am so excited that you are here!

I have a Master's degree in Education and over 20 years experience in teaching, dressmaking and patternmaking.

Generally, my aim with our courses and tutorials @Pattern Academy by Charnold, is to deliver an intensive well-rounded yet simple curriculum in pattern cutting, that offers a high industry standard level and yet incorporates bespoke fitting to individual body sizes and shapes.

Specifically, in this book, I will show you how to draft your bodice / torso blocks using your personal measurements. Creating a block that is exactly suited for your body and shape, will provide a great foundation for making clothes that fit you beautifully.

What you will learn in this book, will help you push past the usual standard sizing and commercial pattern offering out there, which assumes that we are all the same, and you will become more in charge of your own design outcomes.

I believe that "To look the best you, BESPOKE is the way to go"

What Is A Block In Pattern Drafting?

A Block is a representation of body measurements on paper using either standard measurements or your personal measurements.

Pattern Drafting is using your body measurements or standard measurements to draft a block. The basic blocks are; Bodice, Torso, Sleeve, Skirt and Trouser.

In this book, I will show you how to draft the different types of Bodice / Torso blocks and the Sleeve blocks, using your body measurements.

Note that a bodice block is drafted up to the waist while the torso block is drafted up to the hip. Hence I refer to these blocks as Bodice / Torso, as you can get a bodice block out of a torso block.

On completion of the blocks, you can trace each block on to fresh pattern paper, apply seam allowances all round and use to cut out and sew a toile to check the fit on you. You can apply 3/8 (1cm) all around except at hem which will be 3/4 inch (2cm).

I like To Keep It Simple

A lot of drafting methods require you to take so many measurements and this can making the drafting process become more complicated. Moreover, some of those measurements recommended are usually easier to achieve on a mannequin or dress form but a lot more difficult to achieve accurately on the human body.

Hence, in the method I teach in this book, and at our academy, I simplify the drafting process by using minimum number of measurements which are then strategically applied to obtain other necessary measurements needed to achieve a good personal fit. For example, using the bust measurement to calculate for the bust span, the sleeve head height etc.

What will be covered:

The Dartless Bodice / Torso Blocks
The Darted Bodice / Torso Blocks
The Sleeve Blocks

Aim: To teach you how to draft Bodice / Torso Blocks using your personal body measurements or the body measurements of others / your clients.

Learning Objectives:

At the end of the study in this book, you will be able to use personal measurements to:

1. Draft a Dartless Bodice / Torso Block - Back
2. Draft a Dartless Bodice / Torso Block - Front
3. Draft a Sleeve Block for the Dartless Bodice / Torso Block
4. Draft a Darted Bodice / Torso Block - Back
5. Draft a Darted Bodice / Torso Block - Front
6. Draft a Sleeve Block for the Darted Bodice / Torso Block
7. Achieve two sets of blocks consisting of the 6 blocks as listed in 1. To 6. above.

The Bodice / Torso Block Sets

Set 1. Dartless Blocks: Bodice / Torso Back & Front and Sleeve
Set 2. Darted Blocks: Bodice / Torso Back & Front and Sleeve

Set 1 - Dartless Bodice / Torso and Sleeve Blocks

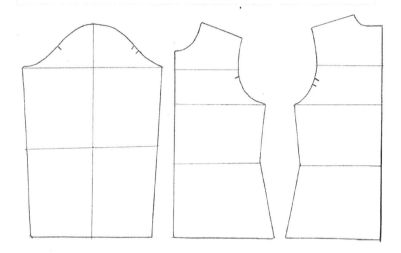

Set 2 - Darted Bodice / Torso and Sleeve Blocks

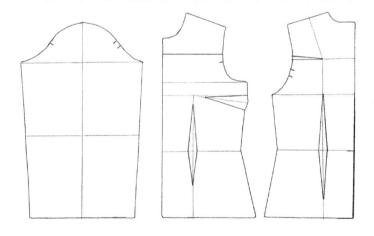

Measurement and Calculation Form

Name: Date:

	What to measure	Your Measurement	Ease amount	Measurement + Ease	Calculation
1.	Bust		Plus 4 inches		
2.	Hip		Plus 3 inches		
3.	Neck				
4.	Back Shoulder Width				
	*For the vertical measurements below, tie a string around your reference points as shown in the photo guide				
5.	Waist to about 1 inch below armpit				
6.	Back Shoulder to Waist				
7.	Nape to Waist				
	*Additional measurements needed for adapting to Darted Block				
8.	Front Shoulder to Waist				
9.	Waist Circumference		Plus 1 inch		

Very important – Wear body hugging clothes on the body to measure, so that the exact outline of the body shows

See the photo guide of where to measure for 1 **to 9, on the next page.

Finally, for the sleeve, you will need only one additional measurement, and that is the:

10. Arm Length

PATTERN ACADEMY
by **CH&RNOLD**

Measurement and Calculation Form

Name: Eby   Date:

	What to measure	Your Measurement	Ease amount	Measurement + Ease	Calculation
1.	Bust	38 inches (95cm)	Plus 4 inches (10cm)	42 inches (105cm)	
2.	Hip	43 inches (107.5cm)	Plus 3 inches (7.5cm)	46 inches (115cm)	
3.	Neck	15-1/2 inches (38.75cm)			
4.	Back Shoulder Width	16 inches (40cm)			
	*For the vertical measurements below, tie a string around your reference points as shown in the photo guide				
5.	Waist to about 1 inch below armpit	7 inches (17.5cm)			
6.	Back Shoulder to Waist	16-3/4 inches (41.9cm)			
7.	Nape to Waist	16 inches (40cm)			
	*Additional measurements needed for adapting to Darted Block				
8.	Front Shoulder to Waist	17-1/2 inches (43.75cm)			
9.	Waist Circumference	33 inches (82.5cm)	Plus 1 inch (2.5cm)	34 inches (85cm)	

Very important – Wear body hugging clothes on the body to be measured, so that the exact outline of the body shows

See the photo guide of where to measure for 1 **to 9,** on the next page.

Finally, for the sleeve, you will need only one additional measurement, and that is the:

Arm Length – 24-1/2 inches (61.25cm)

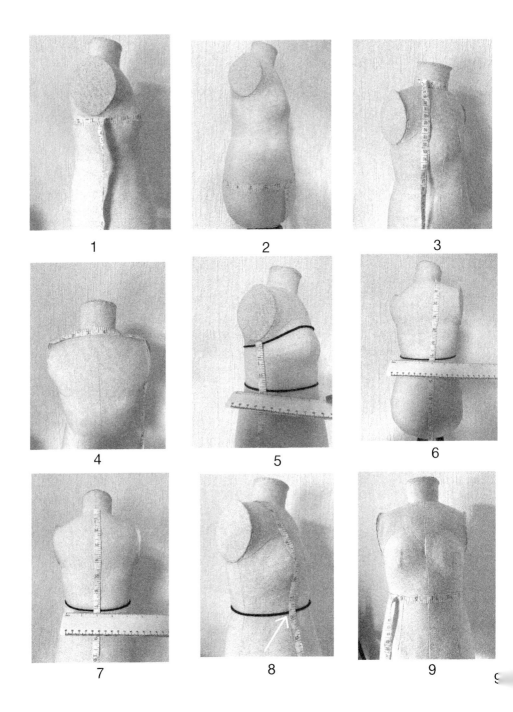

1

2

3

4

5

6

7

8

9

How To Read Tape Measure

Tape measure in inches with _8_ equal sections is read in _eighths_ like this:

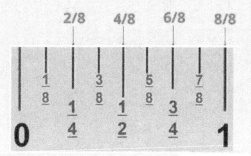

This is a useful conversion chart from fraction to decimal to help you when pattern drafting in inches:

1/8 = 0.125
2/8 or 1/4 = 0.25
3/8 = 0.375
4/8 or 1/2 = 0.5
5/8 = 0.625
6/8 = 0.75
7/8 = 0.875

Fractions into decimals conversion table

FRACTION	DECIMAL	FRACTION	DECIMAL	FRACTION	DECIMAL
1/16	0.0625	6/16 or 3/8	0.375	11/16	0.6875
2/16 or 1/8	0.125	7/16	0.4375	12/16 or 3/4	0.75
3/16	0.1875	8/16 4/8 or 1/2	0.5	13/16	0.8125
4/16 or 2/8 or 1/4	0.25	9/16	0.5625	14/16 or 7/8	0.875
5/16	0.3125	10/16 or 5/8	0.625	15/16	0.9375

Connect with us:
Website: www.charnold.com
Instagram: Pattern Academy By Charnold
Youtube: Pattern Academy By Charnold
Facebook: Charnold - Trainers in Dressmaking
Email: Charnoldltd@gmail.com

DARTLESS BODICE / TORSO BLOCK

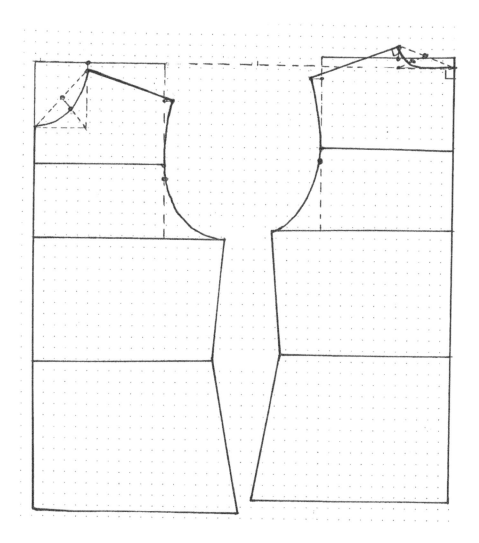

NOTES

The dartless bodice block is generally used to make loose fitting garments. This type of block is a foundation block that can be adapted and developed in patternmaking to create endless designs for both non-stretchy and stretchy fabrics.

I believe that this is the best block for a beginner to start with as you do not have to worry about darts, yet there are endless designs you can make with it.

I advise that you draft your sleeve block for the dartless bodice block alongside and use them to explore and develop your patternmaking skills before progressing to darted block.

Sleeve block drafting is on pages 42 to 46.

**It is important to note, that your own block may not look exactly like the one shown in this book, as your measurements and body shape may be different to the ones used to draft these.

My example measurements used for the dartless bodice /torso blocks shown in this book are:

1. Bust = 38 inches
2. Hip = 43 inches
3. Neck = 15-1/2 inches
4. Back Shoulder Width = 16 inches
5. Waist to about 1inch below armpit = 7 inches
6. Back Shoulder to Waist = 16-3/4 inches
7. Nape to Waist = 16 inches

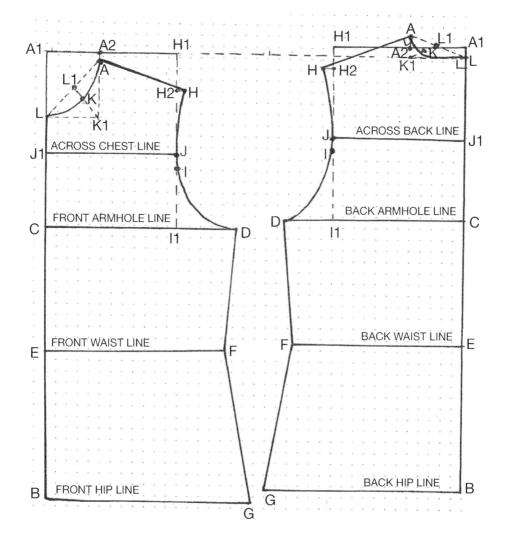

Steps to draft the Dartless Bodice / Torso Block

The Back:
Back Main Frame
A1 to B = back shoulder to waist plus 8 inches (centre back line)
A1 to H1 = half (1/2) shoulder minus 3/8 inch (1cm)
A1 to E = back shoulder to waist, square out a guide line
E to C = measurement of waist to one inch below armpit to get the armhole depth line (C - D)
C to D = 1/4 bust plus ease minus 1/4 inch (0.6cm)
E to F = C to D minus 3/4 inch (2cm)*
*Optional as you can choose not to shape the waist or shape with less amount
B to G = 1/4 hip plus ease minus 1/4 inch (0.6cm)
Connect **G to F to D** for back side seam

Back Shoulder seam
Square down from a guide line from **H1 to I1** on the armhole depth line
H1 to H2 = 1/10 of shoulder minus 1/2inch (1.2cm)
A1 to A2 = 1/5 of neck
A2 to A = 1/2inch (1.2cm)
Square out from **H2 to H**, a distance of 3/8 inch (1cm)
Connect **H to A** for back shoulder seam*
*Take note of the back shoulder seam distance as you will need it when drafting the front

Back Neck:
E to L = waist to nape
L to K1 = A1 to A2, draw a guide line
Join **A to L** with a guide line
L1 = midpoint A to L
Join **L1 to K1** with a guide line
Midpoint L1 to K1 is **K**
Connect **A to K to L** with a smooth curve for back neck curve (ensure 90 degrees from shoulder line and centre back line)

Back Armhole:

J = midpoint of H2 to I1

Go down 3/4 inch from J and mark **I**

Connect **H to J and I to D** with a smooth curve for back armhole curve

The Front:
Front Main Frame

Extend the nape line up to a distance of 1/4 hip plus ease plus about 4 inches and mark front point **A1**

Square down from front A1 to distance of back Nape to Hip plus 1/2 inch and mark front point **B**

Mark front centre line

B to G = 1/4 hip plus ease plus 1/4 inch(0.6cm)

This is the front hip line

Extend back waist and armhole lines to the centre front line (with guide lines)

Drop the back armhole depth line by 1/2 inch(1.2cm) to get the front armhole depth line

Drop the back waist line by 1/2 inch(1.2cm) to get the front waist line

Mark **C** and **E** respectively on the dropped lines

C to D = 1/4 bust plus ease plus 1/4inch(0.6cm)

E to F = C to D minus 3/4inch(2cm)*

Optional as you can choose not to shape the waist or shape with less amount

Join **G to F to D** for front side seam

Front Shoulder seam

A1 to H1 = 1/2 shoulder minus 5/8 inch(1.5cm)

Square down **H1 to I1** on the armhole depth line

H1 to H2 = 1/10 of shoulder plus 1/4 inch(0.6cm)

A1 to A2 = 1/5 of neck minus 1/8 inch(0.6cm)

Square down from **A2 to A** a distance of 1/4 inch(0.6cm)

H2 to H = 3/8 inch (1cm) (extend out a guide line)

Connect **A to H** for shoulder seam (same distance as A to H at back)*

*Note it may or may not fall directly on H

*If not adjust point H so that the front shoulder corresponds to the same distance as the back shoulder seam

16

Front Neck
A1 to L = 1/5 neck plus 1/4 inch(0.6cm)
L to B is the centre front line
L to K1 = A1 to A2
Draw guide lines; **L to K1** and **A to K1**
Join **A to L** with a guide line
L1 = midpoint of A to L
Join **L1 to K1** with a guide line
K equals approx **1/3 of L1 to K1** (measuring from L1)
Join **A to K to L** with a smooth curve for front neck curve**
(**ensure 90 degrees is maintained at the centre front and neck point to avoid any sharp points)

Front Armhole
At midpoint **H2 to I1** mark point **J**
Go down from **J to I** by 3/4 inch(2cm)
Connect **H to J to I to D** with a smooth curve for front armhole curve

**See the diagrams for the steps in the next few pages.

Back Main Frame

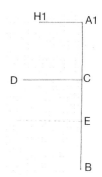

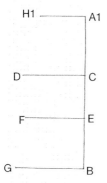
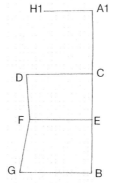

Back Shoulder Seam

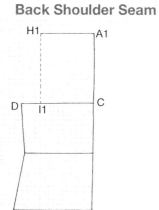
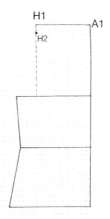
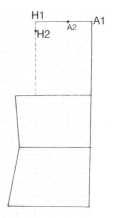

18

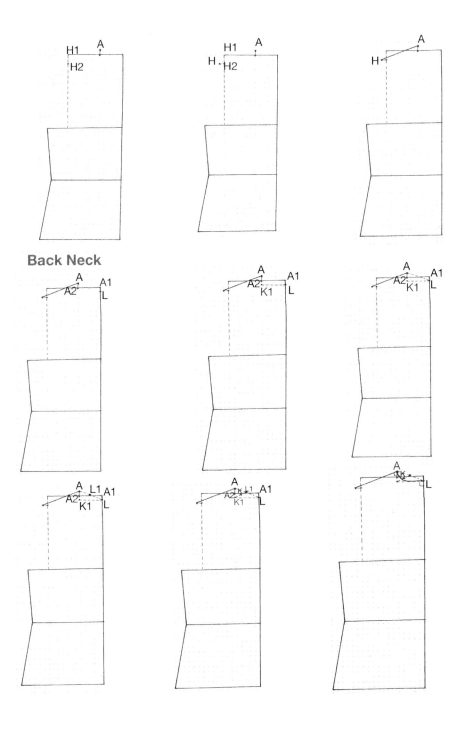

Back Neck

Back Armhole

The Front

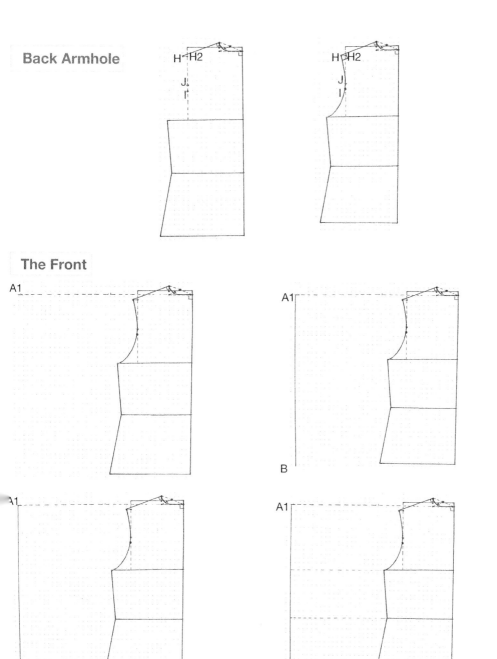

20

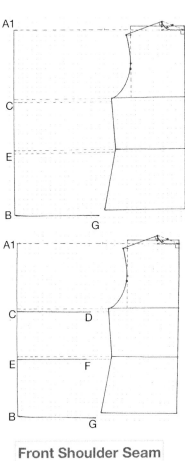

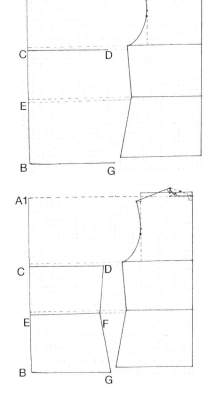

Front Shoulder Seam

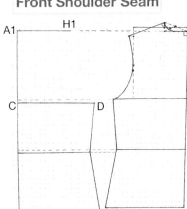

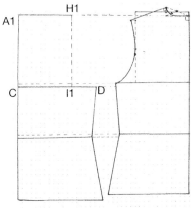

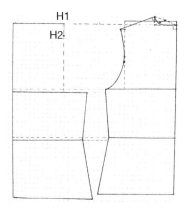

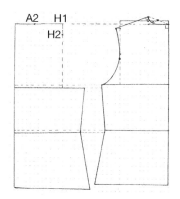

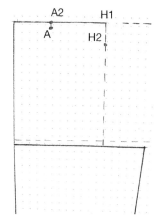

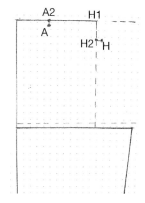

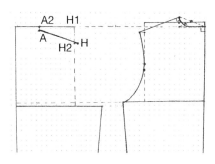

Front Neck

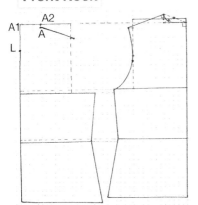

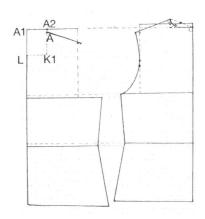

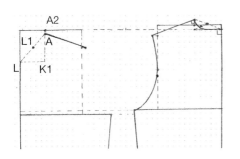

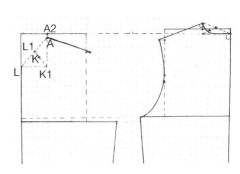

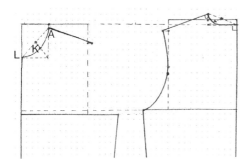

Front Armhole

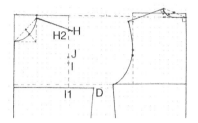 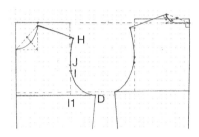

You have now completed your back and front blocks.
Now draw in any outstanding reference lines and label all your reference lines.

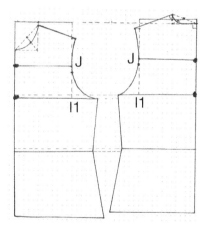

Using the same distance of **I1 to J** on both back and front blocks, square a line from the centre lines to points J on both blocks.

On the back, this is the **Across Back Line**, which is also called the **Back Yoke Line**.

On the front, this is the **Across Chest Line** which is also called the **Front Yoke Line**.

DARTLESS BODICE / TORSO BLOCK

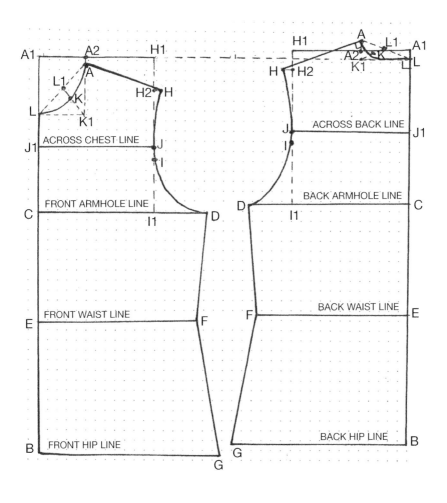

THE DARTED BODICE / TORSO BLOCK

The darted bodice blocks are generally used to make more close fitting garments. This type of block is a foundation block that can be adapted and developed in patternmaking to create endless designs for both non-stretchy (woven fabrics) and two way stretchy fabrics.

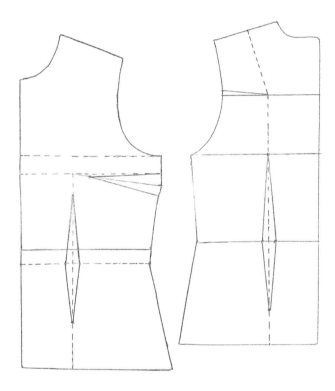

Note that the darts can be manipulated into other positions to create other blocks.

The additional example measurements I used for adapting to the darted bodice / torso blocks are:
8. Front Shoulder to Waist = 17-1/2 inches
9. Waist circumference = 33 inches (82.5cm

To adapt the dartless block to darted block, here are the steps:

The Back

Trace around your back bodice on fresh pattern paper and transfer all reference lines, extending the waist line by 3/4 inch(2cm)
Label related points from the block.
Note that we will create some additional points as we go along, in the process of converting to the darted block.

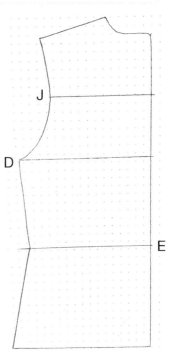

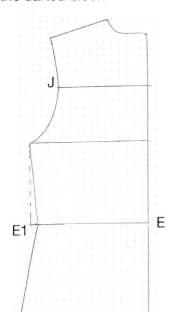

Square down from D to waist line and mark point E1

Erase the previous side
seam.

E to E2 - 1/4 waist plus ease
minus 1/4 inch(0.6cm)

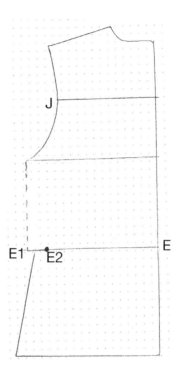

E2 to F - 2/3 of E2 to E1

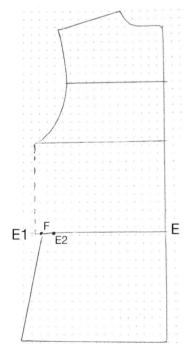

28

Connect F to D and smooth
out the side seam from F to
hip.
Erase any unwanted lines.

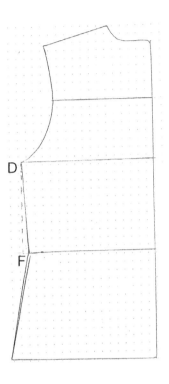

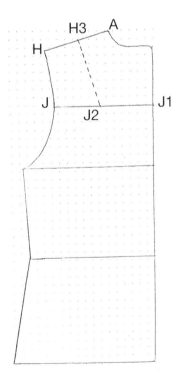

H3 is Shoulder seam (H to
A) / 2 plus 1/4 inch (0.6cm),
measuring from point H.

Square down a line from the
shoulder seam line, from H3
to touch J to J1 line and
label J2.

Go up J 3/8 inch (1cm) and
connect from there to point
J2 for Back Shoulder Blade
dart.
This will also reduce the back
armhole to make it more
fitted.

This dart can later be
manipulated to the Shoulder
as preferred.

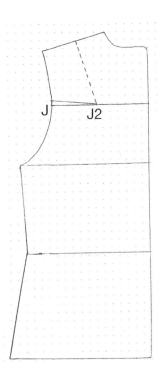

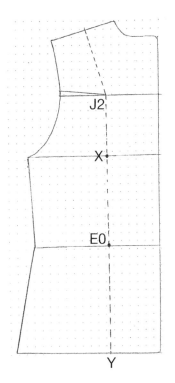

From J2 square down a line to
point Y.
Mark points X and E0 at the
intersections of the lines

On either side of E0 mark half
the distance of E2 to F for the
waist dart.

Go down 5-1/2inches (14cm)
from E0 and mark Y1

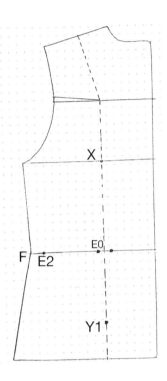

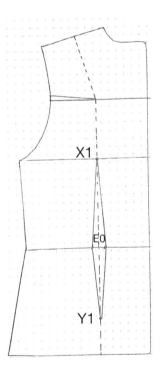

Now complete the waist dart by
joining the points from X to Y1
through the points on either
side of E0 (As shown).

Your back darted block is
now complete.

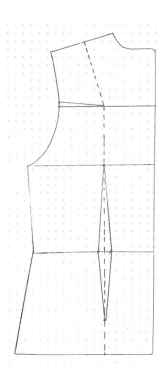

The Front

Trace your front dartless block only up to the waist and mark in your C to D line.

Raise the front armhole depth line C to D by 3/8inch(1cm) denoted with dash line. Ensure your new C to D equals the same distance as the old C to D. This is the new armhole depth line.

Square up a line from the new CD line, touching the edge of the midpoint your current armhole, and up to the shoulder seam line.

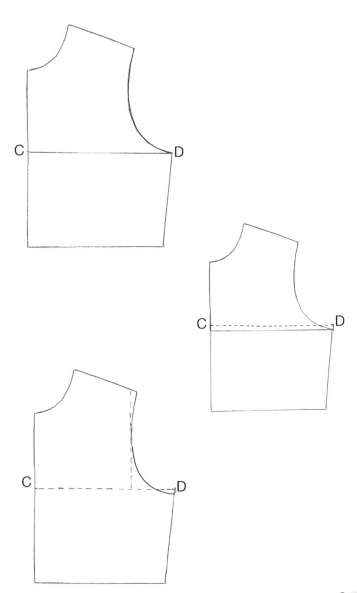

Mark the mid point of this line as J and from point J, go down 3/4 inch and mark point I.

Redraw your armhole to a smooth curve from D to I.

Erase the unwanted parts of the old armhole. Your new armhole is now complete.

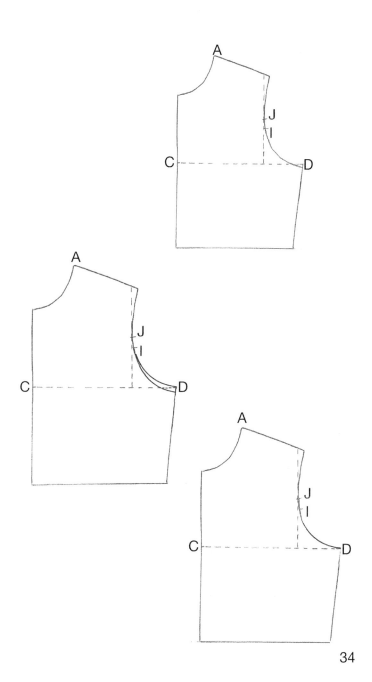

34

Measure and
mark in the front
shoulder to waist
line measurement
starting from
point A and draw
a horizontal line
across. This will
be the new front
waist line.

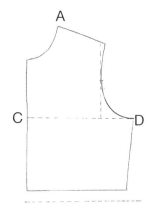

Square down
from the centre
front line and
armhole depth
line to the new
waist line and
mark points E
and E1. Erase the
old side seam.

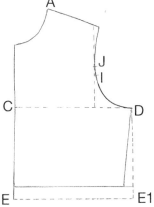

On this new waist
line, From point
E, mark point E2
= (1/4 of your
waist plus ease)
plus 1/4 inch.

E.g waist =
33inches + 1 inch
ease = 34inches
34/4 = 8.5 + 0.25
= 8.75inches.

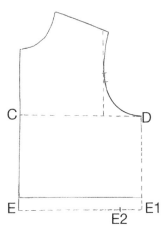

Point F is 2/3 of E2 to E1 measuring from point E2 (This will be your front waist dart intake amount).

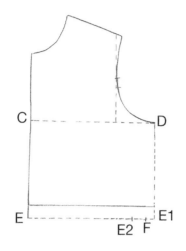

From the front waist line complete the block to the hip line by squaring down 8 inches (20cm) from point E to point B. Then draw B to G = 1/4 hip + ease plus 1/4 inch. Connect G to F.

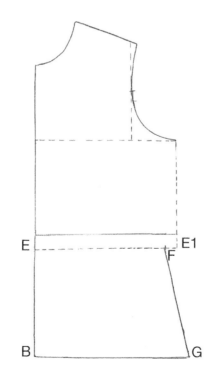

Mark your bust line
C1 to D1(this will
be between 1.5 to 2
inches down from
your new front
armhole line CD).

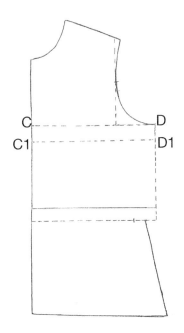

On the bust line C1
to D1, mark a
distance of 1/10 of
your bust
measurement (this
will give you an
approximate
distance for half
your bust span).

Label this point as
X for your bust
point. Mark the
same distance on
the BG line from B
and label as Y.
Join X to Y.
Mark the
intersection point
on the waist line as
E0.

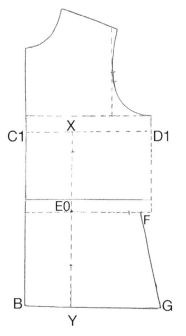

Go down from X, 3/4
inch to 2 inches (2cm to
5cm) depending on the
size of your bust, and
mark X1.

Here I am using
1-1/2inches (4cm)

Go down from E0 about
4-1/2 and mark Y1.

On either side of E0
mark half distance of E2
to F for the waist dart.

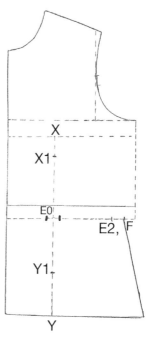

Now complete the waist
dart by joining the points
from X1 to Y1 through
the points on either side
of E0 (As shown).

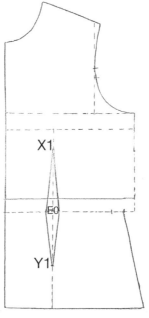

Join a temporary line from point F to D.

Measure this line and mark the difference of the back F to D (back side seam from waist to armhole depth line), as point D2 measuring from point D1*
*(Note that you can also come down from D1 as desired before measuring if you want a more slanted bust dart).

However I advice to measure from D1 for the block and then you can manipulate the dart as desired when making your actual sewing pattern).

Mark the midpoint of D1 to D2 and draw a line from X passing through this midpoint.

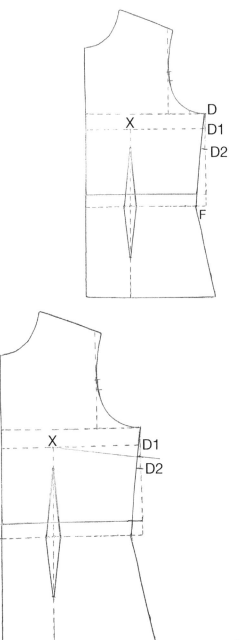

X to X2 = X to X1
Join X2 to D1 and then X2 to D2
for the bust dart legs.

Next, as shown below, fold the
dart leg D2 over D1 (or D1 over
D2 if preferred) then redraw the
side seam from F to D1. Also use
a tracing wheel to trace over the
folded dart.

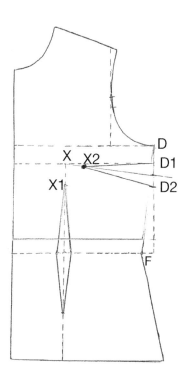

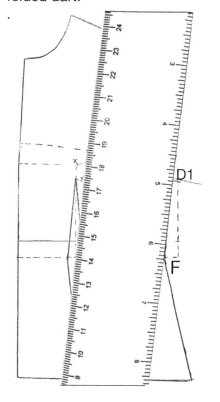

Open up the dart and following the
impression made by the tracing
wheel, complete the dart head.

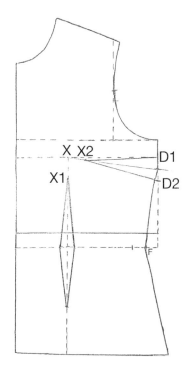

Your darted front block is
complete.

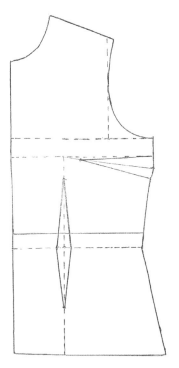

THE SLEEVE BLOCK

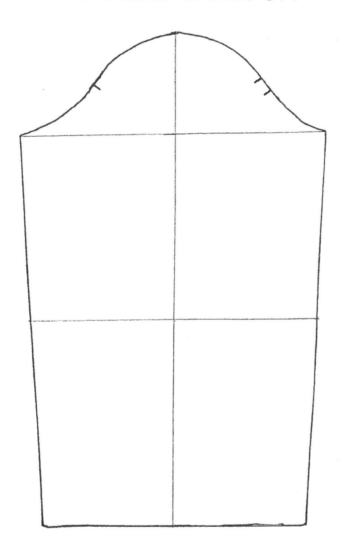

Steps to draft the Sleeve Block

Line A to B - length of arm

A to C - Sleeve Cap Height.

This is calculated using:
1. Bust(without ease) / 10 plus
1-1/4inches (This will give a
medium sleeve cap height).

2. You can also measure from
shoulder tip to the beginning of
your armpit level and use the result.

However I prefer to use the first
option.

**Note: For higher sleeve cap
height, add 1-1/2 to 2-1/4 inches
(4cm to 6cm) to the medium sleeve
cap height.
For lower sleeve cap height,
subtract 1-1/2 to 2-1/4 inches (4cm
to 6cm) from the medium sleeve
cap height.

However, for making the block I
usually use the medium sleeve cap
height.

Mark the front and back.

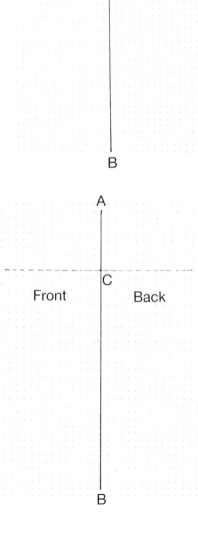

A to D = (Front + Back
Armhole) / 2 minus 1/4inch
(0.6cm)

Place a ruler at point A and
then pivot until the amount
you obtained above touches
the sleeve cap height line on
the back. Mark back point D.

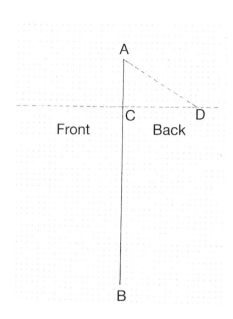

Now do the same on the
front side. Mark front
point D.

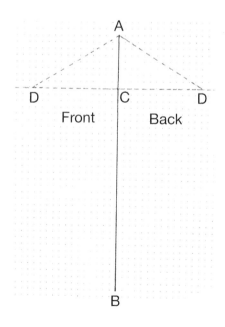

On the back, divide the A to D line into three equal parts, marking points A1 and A2 starting from point A.

On the front, divide the A to D line into 4 equal points, marking points D1, D2 and D3, starting from point D.

A3 = midpoint of A2 to D

Square out lines from the back and front A to D as follows:
A1 = 3/4 inch (2cm)
A3 = 1/4 inch (0.6cm)
D1 = 5/8 inch (1.5cm)
D3 = 3/8 inch (1cm)

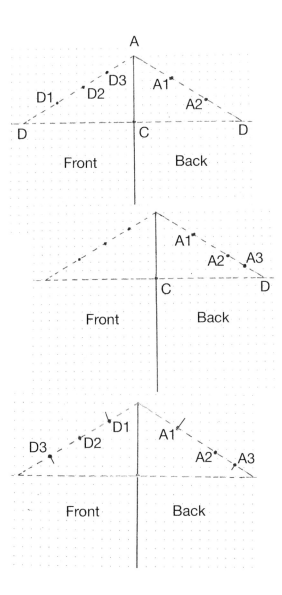

4

On the back connect points A through A1, A2 and A3 to D with a smooth as shown.

On the front, connect points A, through D3, D2 and D1 to D with a smooth curve as shown.

Square down with guide lines, both points D to the wrist level to mark points G1 on the back and front.

Join back G1 to front G1 with guide lines. This is the wrist line.

From G1 to G = 1 inch

Join G to D for the sleeve side seam

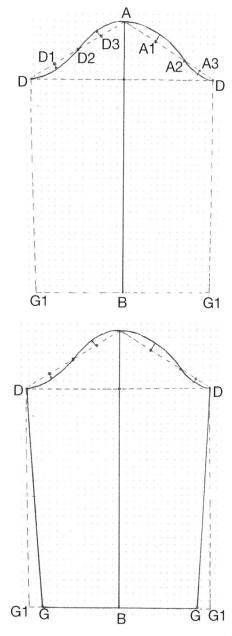

46

C to E = (C to B) / 2
minus 1/2 inch (1.2cm).

Square lines across
from E to F on the
back and front to touch
the side seams. This is
the elbow line.

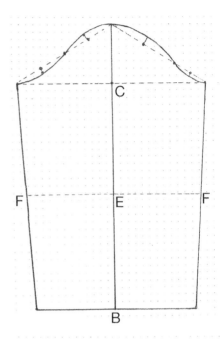

The sleeve is now
complete. Mark your notch
lines:
On the back mark the first
notch line at point A2 and
go up towards A1, 3/8 inch
(1cm) and mark the second
notch.

On the front, mark the
notch line at point D2. The
front has only a single
notch.
Remember to mark in the
same distance of the
notches on the bodice
blocks.

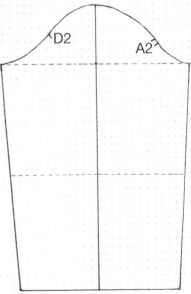

EVALUATION

Did you achieve your 'Learning Objectives'?

Have you completed the following using personal measurements:

1. Drafted a Dartless Bodice / Torso Block - Back?

2. Drafted a Dartless Bodice / Torso Block - Front?

3. Drafted a Sleeve Block for the Dartless Bodice / Torso Block?

4. Drafted a Darted Bodice / Torso Block - Back?

5. Drafted a Darted Bodice / Torso Block - Front?

6. Drafted a Sleeve Block for the Darted Bodice / Torso Block?

7. Achieved two sets of blocks consisting of the 6 blocks?

Congratulations!!!

Printed in Great Britain
by Amazon

23132490R00030